SLAP SHOT

by David Sabino
illustrated by Setor Fiadzigbey

Ready-to-Read

SIMON SPOTLIGHT
An imprint of Simon & Schuster Children's Publishing Division
New York   London   Toronto   Sydney   New Delhi
1230 Avenue of the Americas, New York, New York 10020
This Simon Spotlight edition October 2019
Text copyright © 2019 by Simon & Schuster, Inc.
Illustrations copyright © 2019 by Setor Fiadzigbey
For information about special discounts for bulk purchases, please contact Simon & Schuster Special Sales
at 1-866-506-1949 or business@simonandschuster.com.
Manufactured in the United States of America 0919 LAK
2 4 6 8 10 9 7 5 3 1
Cataloging-in-Publication Data for this title is available from the Library of Congress.
ISBN 978-1-5344-4442-3 (hc)
ISBN 978-1-5344-4441-6 (pbk)
ISBN 978-1-5344-4443-0 (eBook)

GLOSSARY

BLUE LINE: The line separating the end zones from the center ice area

CREASE: The area in front of each goal where players other than the goaltender may not skate unless they have the puck

CROSSBAR: The top post of the goal that holds the net in place

DEFENSEMEN: Skaters who help the goalie by preventing shots close to the net

EVEN STRENGTH: When both teams have the same number of players on the ice

FACE-OFF: When the official drops the puck between two opponents to begin play

FIVE HOLE: The area between the goalie's leg pads

FORWARDS: Players who are usually the teams' leading goal scorers. There are left wing, right wing, and center forwards.

GOAL SCORED: When the puck completely crosses the goal line inside the goal net

HAT TRICK: When one player scores three goals in a game. Fans often celebrate when this happens by throwing hats onto the ice. A natural hat trick is when one player scores three *straight* goals in a row.

ICING: A play in which a player sends the puck from his or her side of the center line across the goal line without it being touched. Because this is not allowed, the face-off returns to the zone of the last player to touch the puck legally.

LIGHT THE LAMP: Another way to say "score a goal." A red light behind the goal is lit to show a goal has been scored.

MAJOR PENALTY: A more serious penalty that requires that player to sit for five minutes

PENALTY BOX: An area across from the team benches where players sit while serving their penalties

PENALTY SHOT: Awarded when a team loses a clear scoring opportunity because of a foul committed by an opposing player. In a penalty shot, a skater tries to score against the goaltender one-on-one, with no help or interference.

POST: The side poles that hold the net in place

POWER PLAY: When one team has more players on the ice because a player on the opposing team is serving a penalty. The team serving the penalty is said to be shorthanded.

SLAP SHOT: A hard shot in which a player takes a big swing before hitting the puck. Some slap shots travel faster than one hundred miles per hour.

Hi! My name is Joe and I am on my way to work at the hockey arena. Today the Polar Bears are playing against the Blades. I am one of the officials who make sure everyone follows the rules.

Come join me! But wear a jacket.
It gets cold at a hockey rink.
Hockey is one of the most popular
winter sports in the world.
Both men and women play hockey
in the Winter Olympics.
Millions of people all over
the world play ice hockey.

Ice hockey is played on both inside and outside rinks.

IF YOU WANT TO PLAY ICE HOCKEY OUTDOORS, ALWAYS HAVE
A GROWN-UP CHECK TO MAKE SURE THE ICE IS STRONG AND SOLID FIRST.
YOU DON'T WANT TO FALL THROUGH THE ICE!

Most people who play ice hockey outside live in countries like the Czech Republic, Canada, Russia, Sweden, Norway, Finland, and places in the United States where it gets very cold in the winter.

This is the Polar Bears' arena. The temperature of the ice is about twenty-five degrees Fahrenheit.

They need to keep the arena
cold so the ice does not melt.
It is warmer in the locker room,
where the players get ready
for the game. Let's head over there.

Hockey players use a lot of equipment. Everyone on the team has a hockey stick and a jersey (or "sweater") with their name and number on the back.

To stay safe, skaters also wear hip pads, shin guards, elbow pads, and helmets with visors or cages, and a mouth guard to protect their teeth.

On their feet they wear
ice skates, of course!
Hockey players are protected
from head to toe.

Hockey pucks are made from very hard rubber and can travel at speeds of more than one hundred miles per hour. If the players didn't wear all their safety equipment, they could get hurt if they got hit with a puck.

Each player on the team has
a special job to do out on the ice.
Forwards are the players who score
the most goals. Defensemen also
try to score, but their main job is
to help stop the other team from
scoring goals.

The goaltenders, also called goalies, have one job: making sure the hockey puck does not go into the net. Since the other team tries to score by shooting pucks at the goal, the goalies have extra-special equipment to keep them safe.

Do you see what the goalie is wearing?
He has shoulder pads, a chest protector, a helmet with a face mask, blocking pads for both legs, a glove on one hand to try to catch the puck, and a blocker on the other hand.

Do you see his hockey stick?
It has a much longer blade than the
ones the other players use.
He uses that to stop the puck
from getting into the net.

There is Stephanie. She works for the Polar Bears. She is the public relations director. Her job is to make sure writers and announcers at today's game have information about the players.

Stephanie knows everything about the players, like how old they are, where they are from, and how many goals they have scored each season in their careers. She even knows the players' family members and friends.

Stephanie is going to the broadcast booth, which is high up in the arena.

This is where announcers describe what is happening in the game to people watching and listening at home on TV, on the radio, or online.

Now let's go down to the ice to see the benches where the players sit during the game. In front of the benches are low walls, called boards, that go all the way around the ice.

There are doors that open,
but many players jump over
the boards to get onto the ice.

On top of some of the boards are tall, clear sheets of thick plastic plexiglass. These help to protect the fans from flying pucks, but still let them see all the action on the ice. Nets above the plexiglass add even more safety for the fans.

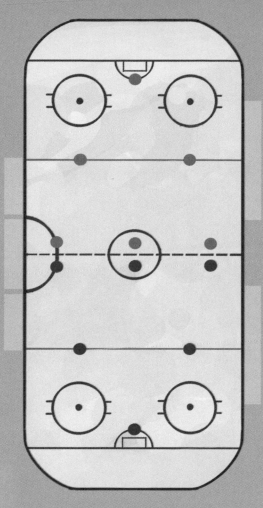

The ice is where the players skate during the game. Although the ice looks very thick, it is less than an inch deep. The lines, circles, and messages that look like they are on the ice are actually stickers *under* the ice, although a few teams paint them on.

To keep the ice nice and smooth for the skaters, a machine called a Zamboni spreads warm water over the ice to fix any bumps or chips. When that water refreezes, the ice is smooth again! Two Zambonis smooth the ice before a game, after a game, and in between each period.

The ice crew places a goal at each end of the ice, one for each team. Each goal is four feet tall and six feet wide, and made of red metal poles and a big net. A goal judge sits behind the plexiglass right near the goal or in the lower stands or press boxes to decide whether a puck makes it all the way across the goal line.

If someone scores a goal, the goal judge lights a red lamp and the team's fans start to cheer.

Sometimes players do not follow the rules and they have to go to the penalty box. That is where *I* work. The players who break the rules sit in the penalty box for a few minutes, like a time-out. When their penalty is over, I open the door to let them back on the ice.

Sometimes players in the penalty box are upset, so I try to make them laugh by telling jokes.

Now it is time for the game to begin. The Polar Bears' and Blades' centers line up at center ice for a face-off. The official drops the puck to begin play.

The Blades' defenseman gets control of the puck and passes it to his teammate.

He skates into the Polar Bears' zone, winds up, and takes a slap shot. The puck goes behind the Polar Bears' goalie. The goal judge turns the red light on. It's a goal!

TEN FUN FACTS ABOUT HOCKEY

1. The first organized game of indoor ice hockey was played at the Victoria Skating Rink in Montreal, Quebec, Canada, in 1875. The first hockey club formed there two years later.

2. The Stanley Cup goes to hockey's best National Hockey League (NHL) professional team every season. Every player, coach, manager, and staff member on the winning team gets their name engraved into the silver bands that make up the Cup.

3. The ice on a hockey rink is just three quarters of an inch thick. That's the same size as a penny standing on its side.

4. Today all hockey pucks are made from rubber, but the first outdoor hockey pucks were made out of frozen cow dung—yuck!

5. "Mr. Hockey" was Gordie Howe's nickname because he was such a good player. He played professionally from the age of eighteen until he was fifty-two. That was long enough to be teammates with his sons Marty and Mark—for seven seasons!

6. Where was the first NHL game played? It sounds like an easy question, but there's no easy answer. The National Hockey League held two games on December 19, 1917, in Canada. One was in Ottawa and one was in Montreal. But nobody knows for sure which game began first! The Ottawa game was scheduled to begin at 8:30 p.m., and the Montreal game was scheduled for 8:15 p.m. But historians cannot confirm whether or not the Montreal game started on time. So we will never know for sure which game started first.

7. The most successful professional hockey team is the Montreal Canadiens. They have won the Stanley Cup twenty-four times. Only baseball's New York Yankees have more professional team championships.

8. Tim Horton was a defenseman and one of the one hundred greatest players in NHL history. He also started a chain of famous doughnut shops. Now there are nearly five thousand Tim Hortons doughnut shops in Canada and the United States.

9. The United States and Canada faced each other in the finals of each of the first nineteen Women's World Championships (1990 through 2018). The United States won nine gold medals and Canada won ten.

10. Wayne Gretzky scored the most NHL goals in a season and a career. Even as a kid, he was a great scorer. When Wayne was ten years old, he scored 378 goals in one season.

AND EVEN MORE FACTS!

Manon Rhéaume was the first woman to play in an NHL game. In 1992, she played goalie for the Tampa Bay Lightning in a preseason game.

Before 1959, hockey goalies did not wear masks. That made it one of the most dangerous positions in all of sports. The man who made wearing hockey masks popular was Jacques Plante, who was one of the first to wear one and who developed many different types. Jacques Plante's first mask is in the Hockey Hall of Fame.